DATE DUE

GAYLORD   PRINTED IN U.S.A.

Slugs Are Gross!

Leigh Rockwood

PowerKiDS
press.

New York

Published in 2011 by The Rosen Publishing Group, Inc.
29 East 21st Street, New York, NY 10010

First Edition

Editor: Maggie Murphy
Book Design: Ashley Burrell
Photo Researcher: Jessica Gerweck

Photo Credits: Cover, pp. 9, 10, 17, 19, 22 Shutterstock.com; p. 4 © www.iStockphoto.com/Sherwin McGehee; p. 5 © www.iStockphoto.com/Henrik Larsson; p. 6 Gerald and Buff Corsi/Visuals Unlimited, Inc./ Getty Images; p. 7 Marc Shandro/Getty Images; p. 8 © www.iStockphoto.com/Achim Prill; p. 11 © www. iStockphoto.com/NickRH; p. 12 © www.iStockphoto.com/Linda Alstead; p. 13 (top) © www.iStockphoto. com/Alasdair Thomson; p. 13 (bottom left) © www.iStockphoto.com/Vladimir Davydov; p. 13 (bottom right) © ARCO/J. Meul/age fotostock; pp. 14–15 © www.iStockphoto.com/Jim DeLillo; p. 16 © www.iStockphoto. com/Sean Jolly; p. 18 © www.iStockphoto.com/Daniel Halvorson; p. 20 © FLPA/Richard Becker/age fotostock; p. 21 © www.iStockphoto.com/Greg Brzezinski.

Library of Congress Cataloging-in-Publication Data

Rockwood, Leigh.
  Slugs are gross! / Leigh Rockwood. — 1st ed.
      p. cm. — (Creepy crawlies)
  Includes index.
  ISBN 978-1-4488-0704-8 (library binding) — ISBN 978-1-4488-1369-8 (pbk.) —
ISBN 978-1-4488-1370-4 (6-pack)
  1. Slugs (Mollusks)—Juvenile literature. I. Title. II. Series: Rockwood, Leigh. Creepy crawlies.
  QL430.4.R62 2011
  594'.3—dc22
                                2010011198

Manufactured in the United States of America

CPSIA Compliance Information: Batch #WS10PK: For Further Information contact Rosen Publishing, New York, New York at 1-800-237-9932

Contents

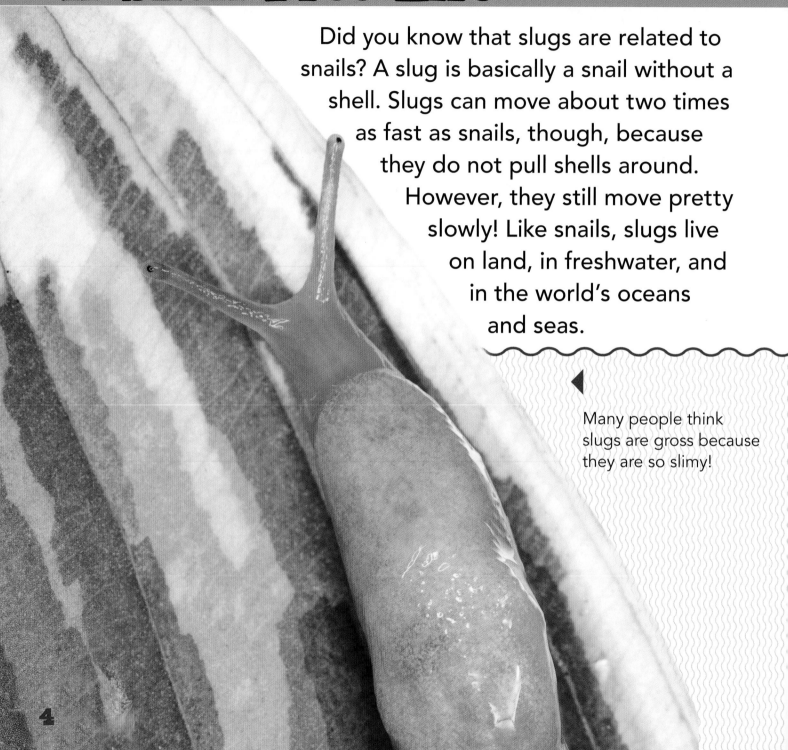

A Shell-Free Life

Did you know that slugs are related to snails? A slug is basically a snail without a shell. Slugs can move about two times as fast as snails, though, because they do not pull shells around. However, they still move pretty slowly! Like snails, slugs live on land, in freshwater, and in the world's oceans and seas.

Many people think slugs are gross because they are so slimy!

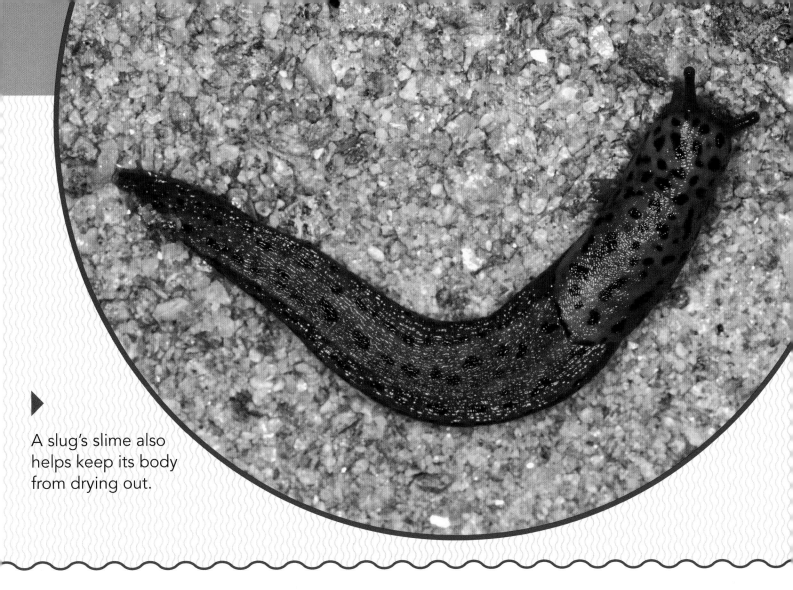

A slug's slime also helps keep its body from drying out.

A slug's body is mostly made up of a head and a foot that wiggles to make the slug move. Land slugs leave trails of sticky slime wherever they go. This stuff helps the slug move. Slug slime can also help the animal hang on to things and can even help it hang upside down!

Soft and Slimy

Slugs belong to a group of **mollusks** called **gastropods**. Slugs have soft, boneless bodies. Since they do not have legs, slugs move by moving their bodies in a wavelike way from back to front. A gland on the underside of the slug's body lets out slimy **mucus** that helps the slug move easily.

Here, you can see both sets of this banana slug's tentacles.

There is a bit of tissue on the slug's back called a mantle. In some species, slugs have small bits of shell under their mantles.

A slug's head is at the front of its body. The slug has two pairs of **tentacles** on its head. The shorter tentacles are used for the slug's senses of touch and smell. The longer tentacles have simple eyes called eyespots. Slugs use mouthparts called radulae to grind up their food.

There are thousands of slug **species** in the world. Slugs come in many sizes. The striped slug is one of the smaller slugs. It is about 1 inch (2.5 cm) long. The spotted garden slug is one of the larger slugs. It is about 6 inches (15 cm) long. Slugs

Land slugs breathe through holes, called pores, on each side of their mantles. They can also breathe through their skin.

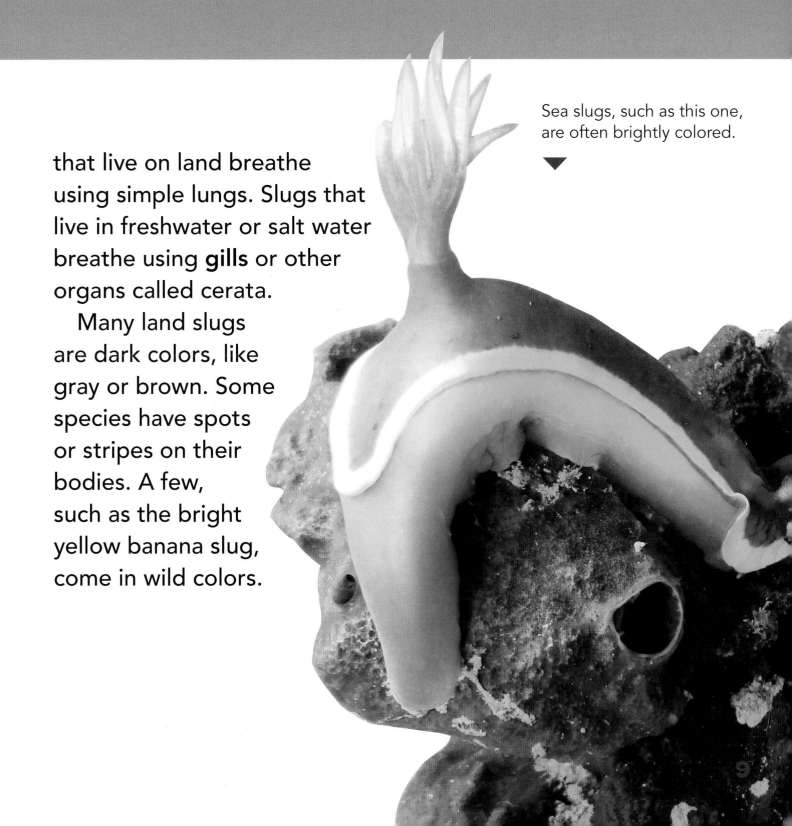

Sea slugs, such as this one, are often brightly colored.

▼

that live on land breathe using simple lungs. Slugs that live in freshwater or salt water breathe using **gills** or other organs called cerata.

Many land slugs are dark colors, like gray or brown. Some species have spots or stripes on their bodies. A few, such as the bright yellow banana slug, come in wild colors.

Land slugs like to keep their skin cool and wet. However, slugs do not have shells that they can hide in when the weather is very hot or very dry, as snails do. To keep their bodies from drying out, slugs stay in cool, shady, wet places during the day. They come out at night or when it is cloudy. Some slugs will **estivate**, or shut down their

Here, a slug crawls over moss growing on a rock. Moss grows in shady, wet places, where slugs like to live.

Leopard slugs, such as the one shown here, are common in Europe and parts of the United States. You might find one living in your cellar!

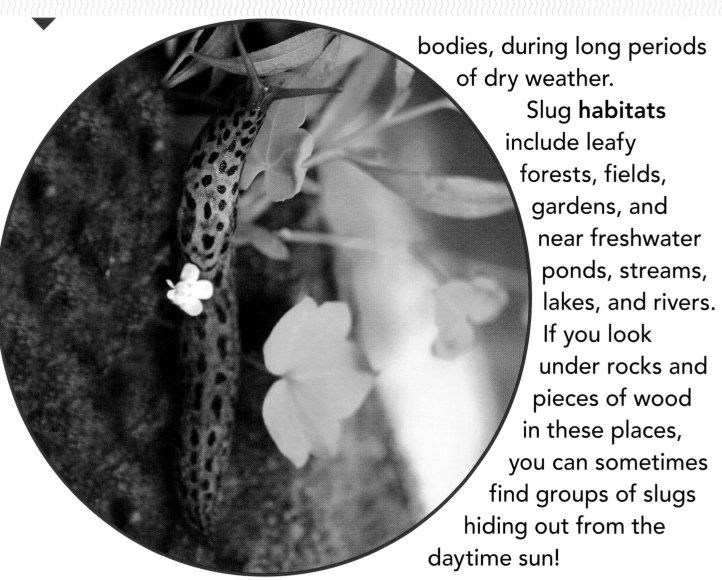

bodies, during long periods of dry weather.

Slug **habitats** include leafy forests, fields, gardens, and near freshwater ponds, streams, lakes, and rivers. If you look under rocks and pieces of wood in these places, you can sometimes find groups of slugs hiding out from the daytime sun!

Life Cycle

2

Like many of its fellow gastropods, most slugs have both male and female parts. That means that as long as two slugs are the same species, any slug can **mate** with any other slug. Each slug helps the other slug **fertilize** the eggs in its body.

1

Land slugs hatch from eggs, as all slugs do. When they hatch, the baby slugs look like tiny adults. They will reach adulthood at around one year of age.

Depending on the species, slugs can live for one to six years if they are lucky enough not to get eaten by **predators**!

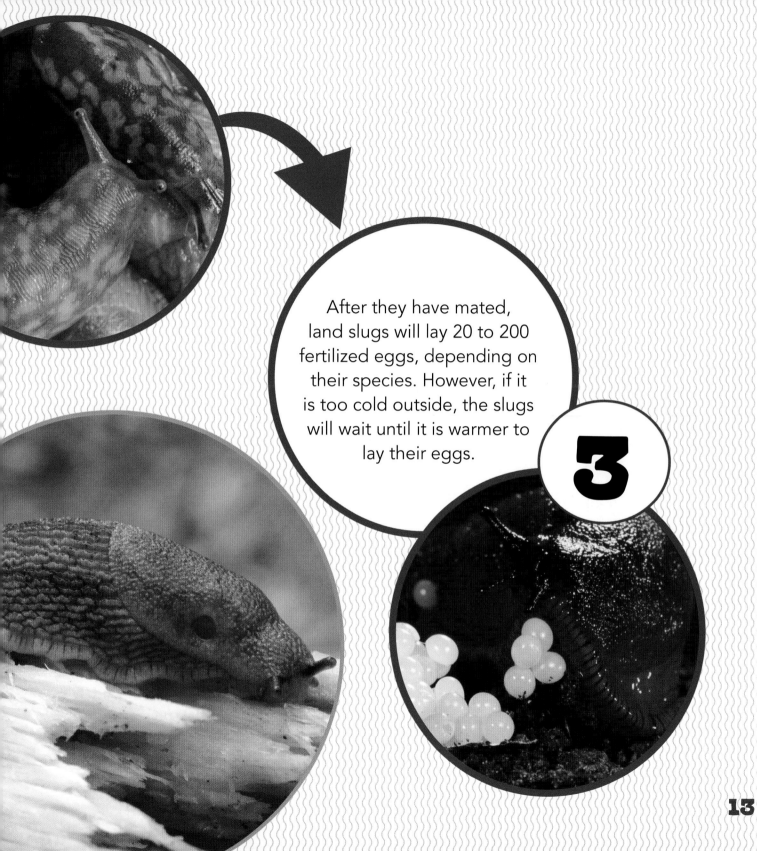

After they have mated, land slugs will lay 20 to 200 fertilized eggs, depending on their species. However, if it is too cold outside, the slugs will wait until it is warmer to lay their eggs.

3

Fact Sheet: GROSS!

1 Banana slugs sometimes eat each other's mucus before mating!

2 Slugs and snails are related to clams, squid, and octopuses. All of these animals are mollusks.

3 Did you know that salt can kill land slugs? Putting salt on a land slug's body causes all the fluid in the slug's body to seep out. The animal then dries up and dies.

4 In some parts of the world, people eat slugs.

At the University of California-Santa Cruz, the banana slug is the mascot for the school's teams. This bright yellow slug lives in the woods near the school.

Sea slugs are brightly colored and are sometimes also called nudibranchs.

On fish farms, dried slugs are used as fish food.

Scientific names often tell you something about what an animal looks like. Slugs are gastropods, which is Latin for "stomach-foot!"

Slug Food

Most land slugs eat dead and rotting plant matter. They also eat living plants and fungi, such as mushrooms. Some slugs are predators that hunt and eat small animals, such as earthworms.

Slugs munch on their lunch using their radulae. The radula is like a tongue with tiny teeth. These

▼ This slug is using its radula to grind up the leaf it is eating!

A group of slugs, such as the one shown here, can eat a whole plant very quickly.

teeth are called denticles. As the denticles wear down from use, new ones take their places. Gardeners do not like to see plant-eating slugs in their gardens because slugs eat seeds. They also chew up leaves, flowers, fruits, and vegetables. The munching, as well as the slime slugs leave behind, can ruin their plants.

The banana slug is the second-largest species of slug in the world. It can be from 6 to 10 inches (15–25 cm) long. Most banana slugs are bright yellow and really do look like bananas! They can also be green, brown, or white. The slug's coloring can change depending on what it eats and how humid the slug's habitat is. Banana slugs live in the western United States.

Most of the United States' banana slugs live in California, although they can also be found in Oregon, Washington, and Alaska.

Banana slugs' slimy mucus helps them slide over sharp objects, such as pine needles, on the forest floor.

Banana slugs eat many different things. Like other slugs, they eat plants and mushrooms. They also eat rotting fruit, animal waste, and even other banana slugs! Banana slugs generally live for one to three years, but there have been some that have lived as long as seven years.

Predators and Defenses

Land slugs are food for many animals. Snakes, birds, frogs, salamanders, turtles, and hedgehogs are all animals that eat slugs.

What can slugs do to keep safe from these predators? A slug may wiggle the end of its tail to scare away smaller predators. It may also

▼ Here, a beetle snacks on an unlucky slug.

Sidewalks can be dangerous places for slugs. There, they have nowhere to hide from birds.

scrunch its body into a smaller shape to try to keep its head safe. The spotted garden slug can even shoot blood from its body to scare away predators! The last line of **defense** for many slugs is their mucus. The slimy mucus makes it hard for an animal to hold on to a slug. The mucus also tastes bad to many animals, which will make them give up on a slug supper.

Many people think of land slugs as garden pests. However, these slugs do play an important part in the food chain. A food chain links all the animals in a habitat to one another. Slugs are near the bottom of the food chain because so many other animals eat them.

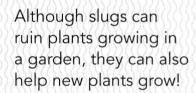

Although slugs can ruin plants growing in a garden, they can also help new plants grow!

Slugs also play the part of **decomposers**. When they eat rotting plant matter, they are helping break it down. This is part of the way **nutrients** get put back in the soil, which helps plants grow. Slugs are slimy and gross, but they have important jobs to do!

Glossary

decomposers (dee-kum-POH-zerz) Living things that break down the cells of dead plants and animals into simpler parts.

defense (dih-FENTS) Something a living thing does that helps keep it safe.

estivate (ES-tih-vayt) To spend a part of the life cycle resting.

fertilize (FUR-tuh-lyz) To put male cells inside an egg to make babies.

gastropods (GAS-truh-podz) Kinds of soft-bellied mollusks that have heads and one foot.

gills (GILZ) Body parts that fish and other animals that live in the water use for breathing.

habitats (HA-buh-tats) The kinds of land where an animal or a plant naturally lives.

mate (MAYT) To come together to make babies.

mollusks (MAH-lusks) Animals without backbones and with soft bodies and, often, shells.

mucus (MYOO-kus) Thick, slimy matter produced by the bodies of many animals.

nutrients (NOO-tree-ents) Food that a living thing needs to live and grow.

predators (PREH-duh-terz) Animals that kill other animals for food.

species (SPEE-sheez) One kind of living thing. All people are one species.

tentacles (TEN-tih-kulz) Long, thin growths on animals that are used to touch, hold, or move.

Index

B
body, 5–7, 9–12, 14, 21

D
decomposers, 22
defense, 21

E
eggs, 12–13

F
freshwater, 4, 9, 11

G
gastropods, 6, 12, 15

gills, 9

H
habitat(s), 11, 18, 22
head, 5, 7, 21

L
land, 4, 9

M
mollusks, 6, 14
mucus, 6, 14, 21

N
nutrients, 22

O
oceans, 4

P
predators, 12, 16, 20–21

S
shell(s), 4, 10
snail(s), 4, 10, 14
species, 8–9, 12–13, 18

T
tentacles, 7
trails, 5

Web Sites

Due to the changing nature of Internet links, PowerKids Press has developed an online list of Web sites related to the subject of this book. This site is updated regularly. Please use this link to access the list:
www.powerkidslinks.com/creep/slug/